WELCOME
WAITERS' WORLD
THE ESSENTIAL GUIDE TO SERVING FOOD & DRINK

JOËL HOACHUCK

Welcome to Waiters' World by Joël Hoachuck
FIRST EDITION

Published by:

Napa Valley, CA 94559

welcometowaitersworld.com

Ordering Information
Quantity sales: Special discounts are available on quantity purchases by restaurants, associations, and others large groups.

For details, contact:
info@welcometowaitersworld.com

ISBN 978-1-7377112-7-8

WHAT THE INDUSTRY IS SAYING

"As a 40-year veteran in the hospitality industry, I absolutely love this book. *Welcome to Waiters' World* provides everything one must know as well as great reminders we all need from time-to-time. I see this book as an essential training guide for new hires and a useful training tool for owners and manager. *Welcome to Waiters' World* would work well in a classroom setting, where questions and feedback can be immediately discussed. Well done and highly recommended."

Kate O'Reilly, Seasoned Restaurant Professional

"*Welcome to Waiters' World* will certainly save us countless hours of training our wait staff. The techniques taught are easy to understand and are sure to inspire our team to step up and improve the service at our restaurant!"

Zachariah Cratty, Restaurant Manager

"Joël Hoachuck really knows his stuff! I started out working and training with him as a waiter. With the skill set I developed I was soon able to grow into a manager. He offers us, in the restaurant world, years of experience that we can learn from and thrive in our careers."

James Darden, Restaurant Manager & Sommelier

DEDICATION

This book is dedicated to all the wonderful people I have met along the way in all the restaurants I have had the pleasure to work in. It is through teaching others that we, ourselves, grow.

I'd also like to dedicate this book to my wife, Barbara, and my children, Pierre, David, Julien and Arielle, who were with me through this journey, providing a warm home to return to after a long day on the floor.

Thank you.

TABLE OF CONTENTS

ABOUT THE AUTHOR

Joël Hoachuck was born December 24, 1959 in the small town of Carcassonne, in the south of France. He was raised by his mother and grandparents until the age of 17. After graduating high school, he joined the army where he spent five years and then joined the French police. France was becoming too small for Joël, who dreamt of travelling the world. He inherited his sense of adventure from his grandfather, a teacher who travelled throughout the French colonies and shared his stories of faraway places with Joël. His grandmother, who was always cooking up something delicious in the kitchen, instilled a love for food that continues to this day. After leaving the police, Joël took a few jobs—as a cook, captain waiter and then as manager of a restaurant in Nice on the French Riviera, where he met a man who changed his life.

Joël was working as a *chef de rang* (captain waiter) in the Hotel Sofitel in Nice for two years when Pascal came to work. Pascal was 35, had been working as a waiter and then manager on several cruise ships for 15 years, circumnavigating the world. After some long conversations with Pascal, Joël realized that if you knew how to speak English and how to wait tables, you could travel anywhere. That's when he took Pascal's advice and sent out a few resumes. Joël landed a job as a captain waiter on the Queen Elizabeth 2 (QE2). On cruise ships things were different.

Dealing with international food and products in a high-end setting allowed Joël to sharpen and expand his knowledge and skills. By chance, or perhaps it was fate, Joël was serving a table in 1990, when he met his sweet American wife of 30 years, Barbara Schwartz (in the most romantic way, during a stop in Cherbourg, France). She was travelling with her grandparents on the ship. He subsequently quit his job on the ship, moved to America, married Barbara and had two children, Julien and Arielle.

Joël's first three years in America were spent in the Washington D.C. area where he worked as waiter and manager in several restaurants—another enriching experience. Joël and his family then picked up everything and moved west to Napa, California.

In 1993, Napa Valley was poised to become universally recognized for its abundance of talented chefs serving farm fresh food paired with world-renowned wines—the convergence of the food and wine industries was about to explode, right in this beautiful Valley. Joël arrived just in time to become part of the journey, an epic culinary gold rush that put Napa on the map of trending destinations for epicureans worldwide.

Joël honed his skills in some of the best restaurants in the Valley. He first took a waiter job at TraVigne, under the tutelage of Kevin Cronin. Back then, TraVigne was the place to go, to see, and to be seen. The food, wine, and service were all amazing. He then moved on to help open Bouchon in Yountville, for the exceptionally talented, Thomas Keller. He started as a waiter but was rapidly promoted to the General Manager position. Joël's knowledge and style helped put this restaurant on track to what it has become today.

In 2003, Joël accepted the position of Restaurant Manager at Auberge du Soleil, a Relais & Chateaux Resort, another renowned Napa Valley establishment. After several years, he was called upon by celebrity chef, Michael Chiarello, to help him open Bottega in Yountville. As General Manager, Joël played a pivotal role in the restaurant's success. He then decided to check out what was happening nearby in San Francisco and spent some enjoyable times at "ame"—a one Michelin star Japanese-inclined restaurant. Joël returned to Napa to work at Farm Restaurant, part of the Carneros Resort and Spa, but soon returned to work with the Moana LL Corporation, former owners of Auberge du Soleil. He is currently at the helm of El Dorado Kitchen (EDK) in Sonoma, California, located on the Sonoma Plaza.

Through all these experiences, Joël has overseen restaurant front of the house teams from ten to hundreds of employees. He has trained all of them. He has seen the mistakes that are commonly made and understands the steps required to be successful in a waiters' world. Through this book, he hopes to share the knowledge he has accumulated from a lifetime of service with the world.

NOTE: If you're wondering about the title, Waiters' World, it refers to a real place, created more than twenty-five years ago. Back in 1995, while working at TraVigne, management realized there was no place where the waiters could count their money and do their end-of-night paperwork. To solve the problem, they built a long wooden counter downstairs in the corridor leading to the red wine cellar. Above the counter, against the wall, was a series of lockable "pigeon holes," where the waiters would put the little orange envelopes which held the tips for their bar staff, bussers, host staff, and food runners. It didn't take long for this counter to take on a life of its own, along with the name: **WAITERS' WORLD!**

WHO THIS BOOK IS FOR

This book is for Restaurant Owners, Managers and Waiters.

By handing each of your employees a copy of
Welcome to Waiters' World
you'll save countless hours of individual training.
Everything a manager teaches is contained in this guide,
including important techniques and tips that
are often overlooked.

For the inspired waiter, already working the field,
this book will put you at the top of your game.
No matter what your level of experience,
the techniques in this book will make you a success
at your profession, anywhere in the world.

• • • • • • • • • • • •

INTRODUCTION

A lot of people assume that waiting tables is easy: You tell
me what you want to eat; I go pick it up in the kitchen; I
bring it to you; you eat it and voilà!, "Here is your check,
hasta la vista baby." But, it is not that simple. At it's best,
waiting tables is an art. It doesn't matter if you are working
in a small breakfast place, a diner, or a four-star restaurant.
Being a waiter requires a full range of talents: discipline,
good communication and people skills, food and beverage
knowledge, organizational skills and salesmanship.

Thanks to the chefs, and to the diverse melting pot of
cuisines in America, the food we consume and the different
restaurant experiences we enjoy throughout this country
have reached an exciting peak. On the other hand, the
service side of the restaurant industry still has plenty of
room for improvement. It is not unreasonable to say that the
food has evolved in a dramatic way, but the service has been
left behind. How many times have you heard, "The food was
great, but the service was lacking"— far too many times,
I am sure. That's why I decided to do something about it:
To share my knowledge and the experience I acquired all
over the world, in the hopes of helping raise the level of
restaurant service in America.

For this to happen, the way we serve people in restaurants
needs to be standardized. Waiters in all restaurants across
the country need to be on the same page to make it work.
There are several hospitality programs in this country that
are focused on obtaining a Hospitality Management degree.
Skills taught include financial accounting, strategic

management, human resources—great skills management must have. But we also need to go back to basics: As waiters, we need to start out by studying the fundamental techniques of waiting tables and satisfying our customers' craving for good service, as well as good food.

This book will teach you how to become an exceptional waiter. I will give you the tools that allow you to understand and perform the art of waiting tables, resulting in the ability for you to make a decent living at it. In this book, you will find what you need to know about the technical skills, salesmanship, and the attitude needed to make the most out of your job. The purpose of the information in this book is to help waiters perform their job well and with confidence. For managers and trainers, the information will provide the necessary guidelines to train your staff, allowing everyone to speak the same language, provide better service, and make the world a happier place!

Welcome to Waiters' World!

A note on gender and vocabulary:

1. In an effort to be gender neutral, we have used the word "waiter" throughout this book.

2. This book uses many terms that are exclusive to the restaurant industry that may be unfamiliar to you. If you don't know a term, please refer to the Glossary, starting on page 77.

SECTION 1
JOB DESCRIPTION

1.1 WAITERS' WORK ETHIC

Respect your fellow employees and your workplace.
You don't impose or command respect; you earn it. In this
business, if you want to be respected, you have to respect
others. Being a professional and "acting like one" is the first
form of respect you must show toward your workplace and
fellow employees. No matter what your position or rank,
always be polite and understanding. Everybody makes
mistakes. Don't simply point out an error. Instead, teach
your co-worker to learn from it, correct the error and then
guide them to understand how to avoid this mishap in the
future. Never yell, curse, or scream at people—it only
serves to create a bad atmosphere in the workplace.

Be respectful of other people's work and space. When
in the kitchen, address people by their title. Call the chef
"Chef" and call the rest of your colleagues either by their
first name or as "ma'am" or "sir." Always thank your
co-workers for their collaboration. They will appreciate it.
If you need to criticize someone, never do it in front of a
customer or a fellow worker; always try to have a critical
conversation on a one-on-one basis. And never forget to
praise a person when they have done something well—
people learn equally from what they do wrong and right.

**Be especially respectful when interacting with the kitchen
staff.** The kitchen staff works long hours for less money,
and doesn't receive as much recognition as you do. After all,

if the kitchen staff makes good food, it benefits you too.
So show them the respect and appreciation they deserve.

Respect your workplace. Keep everything tidy and
sanitized. Start with the wait station. Don't mess it up;
you are not the only one who works there. Don't drop dirty
glasses, china, or silverware anywhere. Put everything back
where it belongs (menus, glasses, china, trays, etc.).
Being organized is a big help, especially during busy times.

Make sure your tables are always squeaky clean. Clear the
empty glasses and any unnecessary items from your tables
(tea bags and sugar wrappers, straws, etc.). A cocktail glass
should be removed from the table as soon as it is empty.
Keep your tables current and updated. As soon as your
customers leave, clear and reset the table or ask a busser to
do it. It's not very appetizing to have to eat surrounded by
cluttered tables filled with empty dishes and dirty napkins.
An effective way to achieve the best results is to look at
your work environment through your customers' eyes and
ask yourself how you would feel about the place and if you
would like what you see.

**Don't chat with your fellow waiters on the floor or in your
station.** The patrons are not here to listen to all the latest
gossip or racy stories. They don't need to know that the
married manager is having an affair with the host and so
forth. If they want gossip, they can get plenty of it online.

No cell phones on the floor. We all know that we all have
a lot of distracting gizmos available to us in this digital age,
but during our shift, we need to forget about them and
concentrate only on the job at hand!

1.2 BE A TEAM PLAYER

The restaurant is a team, a team on which every player has the same goal: "To satisfy the customer." No matter what it takes, everybody on this team—from the chef, to the managers, to the waiters, to the bussers—everybody needs to remember that the goal is to exceed your customers' expectations. The customer sits at the pinnacle; they are the reason for all the fussing and running about.

Always be helpful. Hands In, Hands Out: Don't walk around empty-handed. There are always some clean glasses, silverware or plates to bring back from the dish wash area to the floor. There are always glasses or silverware that need to be buffed. If you are not busy, see if you can help somebody else. "Do you need me to open some wine?" "Can I pick up some food for you?" "Hey George, you're slammed. Tell me what I can do for you." And believe me: In my experience, I have found that people will always return the favor. Please remember this quote from a fellow chef I used to work with: "If one person is busy, everyone is busy!"

1.3 BE A FIRST-CLASS COMMUNICATOR

Communication is essential in the restaurant business. You have to be able to communicate well and with a varied web of people. As a waiter, you are at the center of this web. First, you must communicate with the customer, explaining the menu and telling them what the restaurant has to offer. Then the customer must communicate with you by giving you their order, telling you what they want, how and when they want it. At this point, in order to satisfy your customer, you have to talk to your busser, to the bartender, to the kitchen staff and on to the chef. You are the Communicator. And because everyone around you is very busy, you have to be brief, as clear and precise as possible, and always get straight to the point. Your co-workers don't have time for long stories or explanations; it has to be "bam, bam, bam" and "Let's keep it moving!". . . especially, when you communicate with the kitchen. These people have dozens of orders in their heads. You only have a section of four or five tables; they have a whole dining room to think about. So, don't waste their time with unnecessary discussions; get straight to the facts. Most importantly, always remember to address the person in charge of the kitchen as "Chef." He is the one who makes the decisions and orchestrates the show.

Communicate with your floor manager or the manager on duty (MOD). If you need help with your section or have a problem with a guest, the MOD is the one to talk to. The manager is the one who can find someone to help you on the floor. If the door is pushing you too hard, see the manager. If the customer at table 11 is complaining about the music level in the restaurant, send the manager. If the couple at table 6 doesn't like their table, call the manager: The manager is the person to handle it. "Communication" is the key word here. It's what being a waiter is all about: Having a very concise, efficient, and crystal-clear ability to communicate.

1.4 TIMING IS EVERYTHING!

Timing is another extremely important concept in waiters' world. First, always show up on time for work. I would even recommend that you come in five to ten minutes early. Those five to ten minutes will allow you to find out which section you are assigned to, which busser or back waiter you will team up with, and have a chance to explain what you expect from them. Every waiter has a different way of working and different expectations. If you are working in a restaurant that has a lot of managers, you must make sure you know who the Manager on Duty (MOD) is and if you are working in a large establishment, you want to know which manager is covering your section. Finally, you must know which team is working in the kitchen and who is the chef or sous-chef in charge. You will then know, right away, with whom you need to communicate. Find out the pace of the kitchen; are they slow tonight or fast? I say this because it is very important to know the speed at which your kitchen can work as this will dictate the way you place your orders. It is imperative to adapt your timing to your own speed and the speed of the people you are working with in order to serve your guests in a timely manner. Yes, there are a lot of different parameters to remember!

Managers hold a Line-up before service. Line-up can be a 15-minute or half-hour meeting. Be on time for it! Often management and/or kitchen has a lot of information to convey in a short amount of time. This is when new SOPS (Standard Operating Procedures) are explained, menu additions, specials or new wines on the wine list are described, alerts about VIPs coming in, special reservation notes regarding customer allergies, birthdays, anniversaries, and all other pertinent information about the upcoming shift are discussed.

You are the timekeeper of your section. You control the pace. You need to give the staff, who works around you, time to perform their tasks. And, once again, you need to read your customer well, because, in fact they set the pace. Some people just want to eat and run, while others prefer to linger. So you must communicate with them precisely and organize your time accordingly. Don't allow the service to suffer.

Always make sure that your appetizers have been cleared and the table has been marked before you bring the next course. As a customer, isn't it terrible when the waiter brings your main course while you are still eating your salad? "What's going on with this guy?" "Hurry up, honey. He is going to bring the dessert, and I want to have a chance to taste my entrée before he clears the table!" Remember: You do not dictate to the customer how fast they must eat; you just follow along.

It takes a lot of practice and experience to get perfect timing. But believe me, it is possible. First, watch your customers. Are they eating slowly or quickly? I personally have seen people spend 40 minutes eating a Caesar Salad. But I have also experienced people eating so fast that I have wondered if any food had ever reached their table! Second, as mentioned, be aware of the kitchen speed: How fast can they deliver your order? Third, watch the bar speed. People often forget about the bar. But it is very, very important for the drinks to be delivered in a timely manner, especially when there is a food and wine or drink pairing. For example, it is not proper service to serve the appetizers before the cocktails have been served, even when the customer gave you the cocktail and food order at the same time. Please, please make sure those cocktails have been served before you put in the food order except, of course, if the patron requests differently. In any case, beverages should always be served before the food.

1.5 KNOW YOUR PRODUCTS

"What are the specials tonight?"
"I dunno."
"How is this dish prepared?"
"I dunno, I'm not the cook."
"What's good?"
"Everything." (Except the service.)

Wrong, wrong, wrong. You are a salesperson, and you want to make money, don't you? In order to do so, *you must know your products.*

The menu. Let's start with the menu, from A to Z. You must know the composition of all the dishes on it and how they are prepared—down to the most minute ingredient (many people have allergies, and some have deadly ones). You must also know and recommend the signature dishes of the house, as well as any specials.

The wine list. You must be able to navigate the customer through the wine list and then find and recommend the wine that will pair best with the food they select. I understand that it is very difficult to know all the wines. (Not everybody has had the chance to live in the Napa Valley and sample as many wines as we lucky ones.) But a basic knowledge of your wines (for example, a general taste and flavor profile of the different varietals you have on your list) is acceptable. If you don't know much about wine, until you become familiar with those on your wine list, I always recommend that you pick at least two white and two red wines from the list that you know are good, pair well with the food and make recommendations using those.

The best way to learn about wine is to taste a lot of it and read a lot about it. I am not going to give you a wine course in this book, but there are a couple of books that I highly recommend. The first is the *The New Wine Lover's Companion: Descriptions of Wines from Around the World* by Ron Herbst. This book contains comprehensive definitions of more than 3,500 wine-related terms, and includes charts, tables, wine maps and helpful tips. The other wine book is one written by a renowned Master Sommelier, Andrea Immer Robinson: *Great Wine Made Simple*. This book will give you a good understanding of the world of wine in general.

The bar. If your restaurant has a full bar, you must know every single alcohol, liquor, after dinner drink, beer, etc. available in your establishment. You must know the names and the ingredients of the basic, classic cocktails, from the simple Gin & Tonic to the more elaborate Manhattan.

The environment. It is also important to know your environment. The layout of your building (where the bathrooms and exits are), the history of the building (if it has one), and the stories behind any interesting pictures on the walls or artifacts in the house. You must give your service a sense of place, a sense of belonging. Nowadays, it isn't difficult to know something about anything. With search engines like Google, you can find answers to all the questions you may have: the food origin, what this or that ingredient is, where this wine comes from and tastes like or what the liquor is that you have never heard of. People like stories and love to be entertained. My recommendation to you is to take a copy of the menu, wine list, and cocktail list home and have some fun doing the research ... do your homework! Doing so will certainly pay off.

1.6 SIDE JOBS

It all starts with a solid "mise en place" (service set-up).
Different rules and policies will apply to your set-up,
depending on which style of restaurant you work in and
what type of cuisine you are serving. Side jobs help you and
the team be ready for service. Each job description has a
set of tasks to perform in order to allow for smooth service.
This set of tasks varies from restaurant to restaurant and
will be explained to you during your training. Keep in mind
that a good *"mise en place"* is 90% of the job done: Did you
make your iced tea? Did you brew the coffee? Do you have
enough spoons, forks, and knives? Are your tables properly
and completely set up? You do not want to figure these
things out when the restaurant is full.

There are Three Kinds of Side Jobs

Opening side jobs: Tasks required before the restaurant
opens in order to perform service, for example, brewing
coffee, making iced tea, folding napkins, setting up the
bread station, filling salt and pepper shakers, filling water
pitchers, etc.

Running side jobs: Tasks required during service to
maintain a smooth shift, a high level of service and save
time for everyone, i.e., brewing more coffee or tea,
continuous restocking of glasses, silverware, china, printer
rolls in the wait station, refilling water pitchers, etc.

Closing side jobs: Tasks required once service is done
to clean up the restaurant and be ready for the next
service, i.e., discarding coffee, iced tea, buffing glasses,

china, silverware, folding napkins, restocking beverages, etc. The key phrase for successful readiness is: "Close to open!" This simply means that at the end of the day, when closing the restaurant, you performed all the necessary tasks to be ready to open effortlessly the following day.

1.7 MANAGING UP, DOWN, & ON THE SIDES, INSIDE OUT & UPSIDE DOWN

Being a waiter is being part of a team, but you also need to help manage. Of course, you need to manage your section, the staff members working with you, such as the hosts, bussers, food runners and bar staff, but you also need to help manage the restaurant. Be your managers' extra pair of eyes: Did you notice that your establishment is running low on flatware, china, and glasses? Do you have a brilliant idea on how things could be done? Is something broken? Are the bathrooms not staying clean enough? Go ahead, let your management team know. Everyone is on the same team and everything, every little piece of information and every idea that can help further enrich the customer experience is, of course, most welcome.

1.8 CUSTOMER PSYCHOLOGY

The customer. The customer is the epicenter of our job, the reason to be in business and to perform well. Waiters need to know their customers, even if it is only for a very short time.

Why does one go out for a meal? The first reason, and the most obvious one, is to eat. And then, to relax. For many people, going out to eat is a type of celebration or a form of entertainment. "I don't feel like cooking at home, so let's go to the restaurant." "I want to have a party (or simply get together with my friends or relatives) but I don't feel like facing the dirty dishes, so let's go to a restaurant." As a result, going out to eat often has a festive connotation, and the customer expects to have a good time and remain in a good mood.

It has become increasingly popular to eat meals away from home in America. With families on the run, and little or no time to cook, going out for a meal has become a familiar event.

Just as people go out to eat for several reasons, people have all different types of food preferences. They don't eat or drink the same way and they certainly don't have the same table etiquette. But they all have one important thing in common: They have expectations. No matter the reason or occasion, if they are sitting at your table, then one thing is for sure—they expect the best service you can offer and the best food their money can buy, and they deserve it.

As the population at large (all ages and income levels) began frequenting restaurants more often, minds have become more open. Our guests are ready to try new flavors, be educated by you, their waiter, and they expect you to show them the way. They will often be eager to try a new dish or a new wine as long as you are able to persuade them that the item is worth the trial. This means that you, as their waiter, must know your menu well!

Another thing the customer likes is recognition. They appreciate being recognized and remembered: "Hi, Mrs. and Mr. Jones, good evening. How are you tonight? Shall I bring you your favorite cocktail?" Try to remember people, especially regular patrons: their names, what they like to drink, eat, or even how they like to be served. They will love you for it, and they will be yours forever. (And your tip will reflect that!) This means that you must be very observant and provide very personable service.

Always try to make the customer comfortable – make them feel welcome and at home. Some restaurants can be intimidating for people (white tablecloths, silver forks and knives, crystal glasses). Help them find their way through the menu or the wine list. In two words, help them "fit in."

Read your table. We often find that customers will let us know exactly what they want without even being asked, by simply observing their behavior, actions, reactions and their tone of voice. Likewise, one can coach the guest through a memorable experience. That's why reading the guests, or "reading the table" in restaurant lingo, is very important. This is a skill that cannot be taught, but can be learned through repetitive observation.

The Lunch or Dinner Date

They are all into themselves. They want to be left alone and we, as the restaurant staff, are not part of their experience. Do your best to blend into the service.

Business Lunch or Dinner

Do as little as possible to interrupt. Make sure their needs are met in a timely fashion and answer all direct questions with clarity and conciseness. Again, blending into the service is best.

The Single Diner

Quite possibly the biggest critics. Some single diners may even be professional food critics, on hand to review the restaurant. It is said that Michelin Guide critics often travel and dine alone, so nothing distracts them from the service, timing, food and ambiance. Quite often they are the most silently critical guests. In these situations, timing needs to be perfect. Again, read your guest. Do they want to talk to you? Do they want to be left alone? Do they want to read? You could offer a magazine or a newspaper, if available. Give these guests the experience they are looking for.

Commonly Observed Guests

The Quiet Couple

If anyone can be more hypercritical than the single diner, it is the quiet couple. They don't talk much to one another. They notice when they don't have bread, they notice when their water is empty. They notice when they haven't been offered cocktails or wine. Five minutes between courses easily turns into 10-20 minutes just by perception. As a waiter, paying close attention to timing is essential here.

The Fighting Couple

Watch out! This is a mine field – welcome to the OK Corral! Nothing tastes good when you are angry. Do not take sides, stay away, and recommend simple food requiring little explanation (do not recommend the steak, it comes with a sharp knife!). Definitely blend into the service, be present, but disappear. Do not hear anything, do not say anything, and make it quick.

The Blogger or Influencer

This is the new millennial kind of customer. They are part of our million new critics.They spend a lot of time online. They take pictures of the food. They analyze everything. Here again, your service needs to be seamless. Make sure the presentation is impeccable. Alert the kitchen and manager that you have a blogger on board. Answer all questions the best you can and make them comfortably part of your world. Show them that you are passionate and attentive. Offer to take their picture for their blog.

Commonly Observed Guests

The Cell Phone Addict

Some restaurants still forbid people to use their cell phones at the bar or in the dining room. But, for the most part, mobile devices are everywhere. If your customer is engaged with their phone, try not to interrupt and not to be nosy. Be sure to make eye contact when taking their order to avoid any mistake or misunderstanding. Write down all special requests. Blending into the service and being discreet is a must.

The "New Puppy" or Tender Care

Some refer to these guests has "high maintenance" while in reality they are just in need of a little extra attention. A "new puppy" will wag its tail and play with you if you scratch its belly and play fetch. However, if you leave it alone for too long and don't please it with all your attention, it will eat your favorite pair of shoes and use a hidden corner of your living room as a fire hydrant. The new puppy guest will be your best friend or your worst enemy. Get every request written down, communicated and executed correctly. Run for their table, back and forth, as many times as necessary.

Commonly Observed Guests

One-Upsman

This guest is going to bait you into an argument. They have always eaten in better restaurants, drank better wine, and lived in better places. These are hard guests to deal with. Let them impress you and try your hardest not to play the "I'm better than you" game back with them.

Speed Demon

These guests want their food and they want it fast. They do not want to wait between courses. Again, timing here is paramount to their leaving satisfied. Five minutes of waiting is perceived as an eternity. But you know what? This is my favorite kind of customer as it enables me to turn my tables faster!

V.I.P.

If you must wait on a Very Important Person such as an actor, politician, the President or the rich and famous, don't worry—it's not a big deal. Just stay true to yourself. Don't change your ways. If you are already used to treating each of your everyday customers as if they were a star (and I recommend you do so) it won't be a problem. The only thing I would advise is that you keep the VIP's presence quiet. Don't let everyone know who is there; celebrities do not necessarily want to spend their meal signing autographs or having the entire restaurant lining up to shake their hand. They just want to enjoy a good, relaxing meal like everyone else. So protect your table and keep a low profile.

Customer's Body Language & Signals

A Pushed Away Plate
Take it away, I'm done. The rest of my table may not be finished but I want you to recognize that I have finished mine and you can now take my plate. In this case, it is okay to clear before the rest of the table.

Bored and Eating
Sometimes the portions are large, and people can't finish their entire plate. Because it's in front of them, they will continue to pick at it, often with fingers or just their forks. To move along efficiently with service, the waiter should inquire if they are done enjoying their course and clear it for them, if so.

Guest Looking Around
Definitely needs you! Where is my server? Run to the table (just kidding, please do not run, you may hurt yourself or someone else, just move with a sense of urgency) and ask them what they need.

1.10 WAITER ATTITUDE

Waiters, what about you? Your presentation is very important, no matter where you work, whether at a small Italian pizzeria or an upscale restaurant, you must be clean and well-groomed. Your uniform must be freshly pressed. You must look sharp; I will even say elegant. Avoid perfumes. The customer is not here to smell Chanel No. 5; they are here to smell the food and the wine. The golden rule: Do not wear any perfume or cologne, not even essential oils.

Don't be a show off ~ stay humble. No need for excessive jewelry, a gold ring on each finger, or an expensive watch on your wrist as it could definitely affect your tip. And remember, first impressions are the most important. People will see you even before you open your mouth. They will know if you are a professional by the way you look and the way you move.

Smiling is gold. How often do you hear people say, "I love this person. No matter what, they are always smiling." It's true, everybody likes smiling faces, especially in our profession. I also know it is not always easy. We all have problems in our lives. Perhaps your wife or your girlfriend just left you, or your puppy just ate your furniture, or your fence is falling down. But you know what? The guest sitting at your table doesn't care about that; they are there to have a good time. So listen to my advice: Be an actor. When you step out onto the floor, put on a smiling face, leave all your problems outside, and entertain these people—you are on stage! Maybe afterwards you'll feel better (or maybe not). But, for sure, you'll make more money.

Attitude. Let's talk about attitude. The only acceptable attitude is a happy and positive one. No matter what happens, no matter how your customer acts, it is quintessential to exhibit the best possible behavior and be 100% positive. You're an actor, remember? And it is not in your character's best interest to argue with a customer, to be mean, condescending or inconsiderate, or even to be the slightest bit impolite.

Try never to use the word "no." Positivity is the watch word. If a guest asks for a substitution on a dish, even if you know that it's impossible to have it done, don't say "no." Tell them, with your wonderful smile and your jovial voice, "Let me talk to the chef about it and see if they can do something for you." Then come back, looking like a dog that can't find their bone, and tell them, "I am so very sorry, but the chef is not able to accommodate your request, ma'am/ sir." And they will believe you. They might even feel sorry that you are so sorry. (You're an actor, remember?) They know that you care about them, that you tried to get what they wanted. And most of the time, even if they don't get it, they still feel good.

Of course, there are some exceptions. Some people don't want to be happy—no matter what. Don't let it get to you. You did your best. In the face of all adversity, remain a happy camper. And believe me, at this game, 90% of the time, you'll be the winner.

Always own your mistakes. Everybody makes mistakes (to err is human). Just apologize and fix the problem. And please, never blame your own errors on someone else. You are a professional: you must maintain your self-esteem and face your responsibilities with confidence. At the end of the day, the way we solve a problem and learn from it is more important than the problem itself.

Be friendly, but not overly friendly. Always address the customer as "sir" or "ma'am." (You can use first names if they want you to do so.) Avoid phrases like, "How are you doing, my friend?" It's very tacky. How can they be your friend? They don't even know you, this is not Facebook! And absolutely, no physical contact, please. Do not pat the customer on the back or touch them in any way. Do not initiate a handshake but shake their hand if they initiate it. I've noticed that men will often shake your hand, but not women. When a man shakes your hand, do not turn to the lady with your hand extended. Wait and see if she moves her hand forward. At this point, it is all right for you to proceed.

Always approach the guest assuming that they do not know anything about food and beverages, while remembering not to be condescending. Again—stay humble, watch your presentation, and be genuine and kind with your words.

The customer is not always right! Although we are customer service oriented, there are some limits to this assertion. If your guests berate you, use profanity, scream at you, become aggressive or touch you in an inappropriate way, do not engage but alert your manager right away and in some cases do not wait too long to call the police and have them handle the situation.

Note: Since COVID, personal space boundaries and etiquette have changed. As the rules are constantly being updated, please remember to check in with management regarding the most current regulations. *Don't forget to wash your hands often and stay safe!*

SECTION 2
LET THE SHOW BEGIN!

Quick Check List:

- [ ] Be Early
- [ ] Clean Uniform
- [ ] Good Attitude
- [ ] Notebook
- [ ] Pen
- [ ] Wine Key
- [ ] Lighter

2.1 SETTING THE TABLE

The table setting described below is for a formal, upscale restaurant. Less formal establishments will use modified versions of this set-up. Make sure you know exactly what your restaurant requires.

Where can I find it?

This is the first question the waiter asks when setting out to set the tables in their section. All restaurants have wait stations and/or storage areas; this could be a hutch or just some shelves located in the kitchen. This is where the waiter can find glassware, silverware, china, salt and pepper shakers, napkins, linen, and all the other utensils used to dress their tables. Other essential items required for service, such as water and iced tea pitchers, condiments, sugar, etc., are also stored here.

Before, during and after your shifts, it is very important to keep these stations and storage areas stocked in order to assure smooth service. During your training you will become familiar with the locations of the tools you will need to provide the best experience possible for your guests.

If Your Restaurant Uses Tablecloths, Cover the Table With it

Make sure it is the right size, balanced on each side of the table, clean and wrinkle-free. Some places use placemats; others leave the tabletop bare.

Then the Centerpiece

Flowers, if any, are usually placed in the center. The position of salt and pepper shakers, and anything else your restaurant requires you to have on the table, varies from place to place.

Now the Silverware

Knife on the right, fork on the left. The knife's blade should face the plate. In some restaurants the set-up includes a salad fork placed to the left of the main course fork and a salad knife placed to the right of the main course knife. All silverware points to 12 o'clock, and should be one inch from the bottom edge of the table. When marking your table for different courses, spoons go on the right. The only fork to go on the right is the cocktail or oyster fork. In upscale restaurants, such as those with Michelin Stars, dessert forks and spoons may be placed at the top of the plate, horizontally. Fork handles face 9 o'clock and spoon handles face 3 o'clock. The waiter moves the silverware to their appropriate position, to the left and right of the cheese or dessert plate at the appropriate time. (See illustrations on pages 38 and 39.) For balance and harmony sake, one customer's main course knife and fork should line up with the other customer's fork and knife sitting opposite them. Always handle silverware by the handle.

Then Comes the Glasses

First on the top and slightly to the right of the main course knife will come the water glass. Going from right to left, the champagne glass is directly above the main course knife. Then comes the white wine glass, followed by the red wine glass, and finally the dessert wine glass (on the far left). This is the traditional glass placement, but may vary from one establishment to another. Always handle glasses by the stem and if not the stem by the bottom of the glass. It is very important not to put your fingers where the guests are going to put their lips.

If a coffee cup is required, it is usually placed to the right of the main course knife, on a saucer with the handle at 4 o'clock and one inch from the table's bottom edge. The coffee

spoon is placed to the right of the cup on the saucer with
the handle against the cup handle and pointing to 4 o'clock
as well. {TIP} *Remember, always handle cups by the handle.*

And the Plates

The bread and butter plate will be placed on the left side of
the fork, (space allowing) one inch from the table's bottom
with the butter knife placed in the plate's center, left or
right side.

Some restaurants have a 12-inch service plate or charger
placed between the knife and the fork. If they do, the folded
napkin will usually be placed on this plate. If there is no
plate or charger, then the napkin will usually be placed
between the knife and the fork. The napkin's fold and
placement may change from place to place. Do not hold the
plates by the rim (to avoid fingerprints). Instead, place your
hand under the plate with your thumb alongside for balance.

NOTES

2.2 FORMAL TABLE SETTING

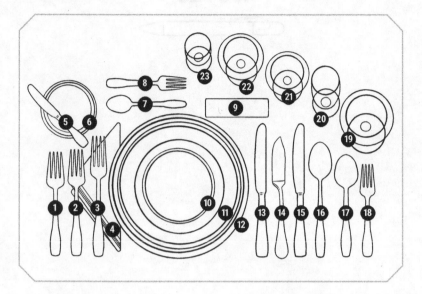

1. Salad Fork
2. Fish Fork
3. Dinner Fork
4. Napkin
5. Butter Knife
6. Bread Plate (B&B)
7. Dessert Spoon
8. Dessert Fork
9. Placecard
10. Salad Plate
11. Soup Bowl
12. Dinner Plate (Charger)

13. Dinner Knife
14. Fish Knife
15. Salad Knife
16. Soup Spoon
17. Teaspoon
18. Oyster/Cocktail Fork
19. Water Glass
20. Champagne Flute
21. White Wine Glass
22. Red Wine Glass
23. Dessert Wine Glass

2.3 BASIC TABLE SETTING

3. Dinner Fork   **13.** Dinner Knife

4. Napkin   **19.** Water Glass

Note: Most restaurants use the basic set-up as illustrated above: a napkin, positioned between a main course knife, and a main course fork with a water glass to the right and slightly above the knife.

Many high-end restaurants do not use the formal set up depicted in the illustration on page 38 anymore, but it is helpful to see it as it will help you know where each piece of silverware, china and glasses must be set. In any case, make sure that each item used in your set-up has been buffed and is clean.

2.4 SEQUENCE OF SERVICE

Table and Position Numbers

Now is a good time to talk about position numbers. In most restaurants, table numbers and position numbers are the only way to locate a guest, both used to place food and drink orders. They indicate the geolocation of your guests, just like Google Maps.

Table numbers are assigned by the restaurant and always remain the same. You can see the table numbers displayed on your POS system when entering an order.

Position numbers are the numbers assigned to each guest at the same table. For example, some restaurants decide that for each table, the guest turning their back to the entrance door will be in position one. From there, we move clockwise with the person to their left in position two and so on. Other restaurants will decide that position one is the person with their back to the kitchen.

Table and position numbers change from restaurant to restaurant. It is always wise to ask your manager for a floor plan so that you can familiarize yourself with your restaurant's table and position numbers before you begin service.

Approach the Table

The customers have just been seated by the host or maître d', and in most cases, have been given the menus; if not, you will have to do so. Always remember that people have their own personal space and are sensitive to having others enter it. Don't approach too quickly. Let them notice that you are coming closer; only after they realize your presence should you begin to talk. Approach slowly, stop so that they acknowledge you, and then move in. Never interrupt a conversation between customers. If they don't take notice of you after entering their space, just come back later.

Observe the Table

Count how many people there are, including how many children, so that you can bring them the appropriate number of menus along with a cocktail and wine list, if your restaurant offers one. Make sure the menus, cocktail and wine lists are in order. Check that you have the menu for the correct day, especially when daily specials are printed. Check the condition and cleanliness of the menus. I know this is usually the host's side job, but it never hurts to double check. It's no fun for the customer to handle an oily or sticky menu or wine list in which half of the pages are missing.

Standing to the right of the guest, starting with the oldest woman, open the menu or present it, as is, if it does not require opening. Continue doing so with all women at the table and then the men starting with the oldest. You then can place the cocktail list and wine list in the middle of the table or hand it to the table's host (this is usually the person who made the reservation). In some high end establishments, it is the norm to unfold the napkin and place it on the lap of the guests before handing them the menu (usually following "the oldest woman first rule," standing to the right of the guest and moving clockwise). This rule applies to parties up to four. Over four, it is acceptable to start with the oldest woman at the table and simply proceed clockwise, regardless of age and gender.

Greet the Guests

"Hi, honey, my name is Gilda, and guess what? I'll be your waiter tonight. So if you don't need anything, let me know." Kind of old-fashioned, overly friendly and a bit rude, wouldn't you say? Your greeting has to be a bit more formal. Nowadays, it's best to skip your name. If they really want to know, they will ask for it, and then they will remember it. I recommend something in the style of, "Good morning, (afternoon or evening). How are you today?" This is a good time to start establishing eye contact with your customers so they realize that you really care about their well-being and are sincere. {TIP} *A good tip on how to establish thorough eye contact: when looking at somebody in the eyes, ask yourself what color they are. The time it takes to notice someone's eye color allows you to establish sufficient eye contact.*

If you know the patron's name, call him or her by it; they will love it. Avoid questions such as, "How may I help you?" or "What can I do for you?" Instead, engage in conversation about water, cocktails, wine and food. Now is the time to start reading your table. Let's get started.

Water Service

Once the table has been greeted, this is the first thing we offer the customer. In some of the places I've managed, the host or person seating the guest asks about water and passes the information on to the busser, or writes the information on the water chart for the busser, barista or waiter to serve. It's now time to start selling. A good way is to ask: "Which kind of water would you prefer today? Iced water or bottled water?" If they opt for bottled, then the next question is: "still or sparkling?" You, your busser or server assistant will then pour the bottled or tap water, as requested. Note that in some states and restaurants, during a drought season, it is a common and acceptable practice not to offer water but to wait for the guest to ask for it. Usually, these kinds of restaurants have a note on their menu making the customer aware of this.

Kid Service

If the table has kids, focus on them. "Let me bring some bread right away for the little ones." "On the menu we have these items which I recommend for children." "If you want me to place an order for the kids right away, please let me know." Bring them crayons, paper, or whatever your restaurant has to offer to keep them entertained. Always ask if a high chair or booster chair is needed. Don't forget the eco-friendly straw for their drinks, the extra napkins, and the "share plates" if they want to try their parents' food. The parents will be eternally grateful for the attention you pay to their youngsters.

Where to Start?

When you have multiple sized parties within your section — a table of two, a table of eight, a table of five — always start with the smallest party first. Two people ask fewer questions than five, and five people ask fewer questions than eight, and so on. So, organize your precious time!

Take the Drink Order

"Would you like a glass of wine, a cocktail, or a soft drink?" "We are offering a special martini tonight." You have just started to take an order. Rule number one: Don't make any assumptions about what they want. Ask all the questions necessary about this order so you get it right. Do they want their cocktail on the rocks or up? Do they want their martini with gin or vodka? Would they like a twist, some olives, or onions in their martini? Do they have a favorite brand? Encourage the customer to be precise about what they want from the beginning and always, always repeat the order back to them. Your guest will be amazed at your efficiency and realize from the beginning that they are dealing with a professional. Get the order complete the first time and you will save a lot of unnecessary running around. (And you will avoid being in the weeds!) Next, ask them if they would like an appetizer to complement their drink: "Would you like a plate of burrata with grilled bread to go with your martini?" It is at this point the customer begins to relax and leaves the meal to the waiter. And trust me, if you put the customer in your pocket, you put their wallet in your pocket too.

Ring the Beverage Order Up & Then Pick it Up

Proceed to your Point of Sales system (POS) and ring up your beverage order. There are many different brands of POS systems out there such as Micros, Aloha, Toast and Squirrel. No one can be expected to know the finer points of all of them. If anything confuses you about the POS system in your restaurant, be sure and get clarification from the get-go, to avoid problems down the line.

When you pick up your drinks, make sure your order is correct. {TIP} *If the drink order is large, imagine that your tray is your table, and set your drinks in the corresponding position numbers — from position one to the last position, clockwise.* (Yes, you need to remember that most of the time in the restaurant business we work clockwise.) That way, you will avoid a lot of confusion, embarrassment and save time.

Let Them Know the Specials for the Day

Let's talk about food. This is the time to display your knowledge. If the specials are written on the menu, show your customers where they are and describe them. Be sharp, clear, and sincere. Use the proper verbiage to make the food appealing to the guest, but don't go on forever. Don't forget that you have other tables to take care of but let them know that if they have questions about anything you will be glad to answer them. {TIP} *If the specials are not on the menu, make sure to let the customer know what they are and, importantly, how much they cost. It can be embarrassing for someone to have to ask for prices in front of the rest of the table.*

When is the proper time to "special" a table? When people ask for it, of course. Some people like to know as soon as they sit down. If it's your choice on when to do it, let's consider different kinds of situations.

Situation 1: When you first approach the table and ask the guest if they want a drink, they let you know that they are going to order a bottle of wine and they know which kind of wine they would like. In this case, I would go get the wine and "special" the table while I'm opening and serving it — making sure to note some of the dishes that match the wine.

Situation 2: The customers would like to start with cocktails. I would first take the order and serve the cocktails and then ask the customer if they are ready to hear about the specials.

Situation 3: The guest wants to order some wine but wants to choose their food first to pair some wine with it. I would "special" them right away and then make some food and wine pairing recommendations.

Always Make Sure They are Ready to Listen to You

Don't be impolite. If you approach a table at a time when people are in a deep conversation and they ignore you, don't interrupt. Come back later.

Make Recommendations

Often times, people coming into your restaurant are first-timers and aren't familiar with your menu. That's why it is always important to make food and beverage recommendations. The best opportunity to do this is when you explain the specials of the day. Many restaurants have one or more signature dishes that are good and have been on their menu for an extended period of time, or a special that you know is awesome. Recommend those. There is a good chance that people will order them and be pleased with their selection. If you can pair a good wine to match the tasty food, that's it! You win! Even your best repeat customers appreciate recommendations. Yes, I know, they come often and might know the menu as well as you do; but guess what? They may grow tired of always eating the same dishes. Point them to new menu items, sell them on the specials of the day, and encourage them to try something new and exciting.

One thing that you want to avoid when making recommendations is greed. You don't need to recommend the most expensive dishes or wine to boost your sales. Try to offer the best choice for your customer based on taste, quality and value. Believe me, when a customer is very happy, no matter how much the check is, the tip will be big.

Another aspect of your job is guest education. I've always thought that it is a clever idea to introduce your guests to new flavors and dishes, especially when you are working with a creative chef. Persuasion is the word. That is what a good salesperson is: someone who can persuade a customer to buy a product with his eyes wide shut. I used to work with a waiter named Murph. He built up so much self-confidence during his years in the business that he was able to walk to a table, take the menus away, without the customers having looked at them, and order the meal for them. When people talked about Tra Vigne (the place where he and I were working together at the time), they often recommended that guests request him. And that is it—he made his customers happy! But for this kind of service, you need knowledge. This knowledge will bring confidence, and this confidence will translate into sales and great tips.

The bottom line is the Two-Minute Rule: you should greet your guests within two minutes of their being seated in your section. Although it is not always easy, you should try to stick to this rule. A simple, "I'll be right with you." goes a long way. Customers feel so much better when they can put a face or a name to their waiter as soon as possible. It lets them know that their presence has been acknowledged. That is why your constant presence in your section is mandatory. Except for when you are running food or getting something in the kitchen, you should be on the floor at all other times, either greeting people or taking care of your customers. Like a bee going from flower to flower, you should go from table to table, making sure everything is fine and everyone is happy.

Take the Food Order

When is the appropriate time to go back to your table and take the food order? As soon as possible! Just keep in mind: YOU control the pace. If you start out at a slow pace, using more time than necessary greeting the table, letting them know the specials, taking the orders, and putting the orders in, and then suddenly try to rush your customers at any time during their meal to make up for lost time, you are going to have unhappy customers. But if you start fast, you will finish fast, and they will follow your speed. Which means be consistent; Be on it! {TIP} *Your goal is to turn your tables as fast as you can, giving the best service without having your guests feel rushed.* (Piece of cake, isn't it?) So go back to that table and ask them if they are ready to order and if they are, go ahead. Please note that an important question to ask before taking the food order is: "Do you have any kind of allergy or food aversions?" This is a very important question which will help you help them navigate their food selection.

As always (and I will keep saying this throughout this book), start with the women (from oldest to youngest) followed by the men (from oldest to youngest). Of course, for large parties (more than four guests), it is acceptable to start with the person in position one and go around the table clockwise. For each person, write down their appetizer, salad, main course, and/or side dish order, if any. If there are multiple courses, be sure to serve them in precisely the order in which they want them. Never assume how they want to eat; Ask them. "Do you want the soup or the salad first?" "Do you prefer to have your salad at the same time, or after your main course?" At this point, it is not necessary to take the dessert order (except if your restaurant offers desserts which take a long preparation time such as soufflés, for example). If your table decides to share a few appetizers or main courses, make sure to ask them if they want you to "course" them, meaning to send those dishes out one by one. Recommending this method works especially well when they are at a small table not able to accommodate many dishes. Once you have the customer's order, collect the menus and bring them back to the menu box at the wait station, or better yet, the host stand.

Put the Food Order In

Now that you have the order, communicate it to the kitchen. Before the computer era (and to this day in some small restaurants) everything was processed by hand. The order was written on a carbon copy and handed to the chef. Now, if you have a POS, you need to punch your order in. There are basically two ways to do it. Some restaurants want you to enter the complete order (appetizer, soup, salad, main course, and sometimes dessert) at the same time. This way, they'll know everything in advance, allowing them to be ready (especially with the items that take a longer time to cook). In some cases, it may be up to you to remind the kitchen to fire up the next course. Usually, you'll find an option key in the POS which says "fire apps" or "fire first course" or "fire main," (whichever may be programmed in your particular computer system). Other systems, such as Micros, will allow you to enter the whole order and put some items on "hold." In this case, it is your responsibility to remove the "hold" when the time comes to fire it up. This sends only the active items to the kitchen. Remember to use the "hold" function appropriately (not forgetting to "unhold" it), so as to keep your timing on track.

The other method of ordering is called "break courses" or "order fire." In these cases, enter the first course on your POS to send it to the kitchen. Then, when you think the timing is right, go back and put the order in for the second course, and so on. Either way, make sure you use all the modifiers your computer system offers. The goal is to communicate the customer's order to the kitchen through your POS with accuracy and precision without having to talk to the chef, which saves everybody time. Make sure you input the customer's position numbers correctly, designating who are women (as they are usually served first), specifying the cooking temperature, if any (rare, medium-rare, medium,

medium-well, or well-done), and any other special requests your POS allows you to enter. If there is any information that your computer does not allow you to type in, just type "see server," then immediately approach the line and communicate your customer's request to the expeditor or the chef, who will in turn write it down on the ticket. Remember: when you approach the line, you need to communicate quickly, clearly, and accurately.

Serving the Food

If your restaurant offers bread, now is the time to serve it, either in a basket that you place in the center of the table or English style, to each individual customer. Make sure it is the freshest bread your restaurant has to offer, with butter, olive oil or whatever your establishment serves with it.

Next, mark the table with the appropriate silverware for their food order (spoon for soup, appetizer/salad fork and appetizer/salad knife for appetizers and salad, cocktail fork and so on). Clearing and crumbing your table between each course is also a must. Table maintenance must be observed at all times. Keep an eye on the kitchen line where the food will come up. Some restaurants have food runners that will run, or deliver, the food to the customer for you. Some restaurants do not. And others use a combination of servers and food runners to get the food out. Usually the food takes between 15–30 minutes to cook, depending on the dish. Check the line often. When the food is ready, clean the rim of each plate with a wiper (usually provided by the expediter) and deliver the food to the table. If the plate is hot, use a cloth napkin to carry it. {TIP} *Remember to avoid putting your finger on the top of the plate rim. Instead, hold it from the bottom with your thumb placed on the side of the rim to balance.* Keep in mind that you serve from the left and clear

from the right. This means that you serve the customer
from their left side using your left hand, and clear from
their right side using your right hand. This is referred to as
serving "open" since we are not closing off the space
between us, avoiding elbowing them. Note: When it is not
feasible to serve from the left and clear from the right, adapt
and serve from the right or clear from the left. No matter
which you do, always remember to serve "open."

For smaller parties, serve the oldest woman first, then the
oldest man. For parties over four, start with position one
and go around clockwise. Do not attempt to carry more than
three plates at once, no stacking, right? Upscale restaurants
prefer that you carry just two plates at a time, one in each
hand. When you have food that will be shared, place the
plate in the center of the table with the appropriate serving
utensils (you should have placed those serving utensils,
usually a large spoon and fork, in the center of the table
when you marked it). Once the food has been dropped, ask if
there is anything else you can bring. Finally, make sure that
all the condiments and dipping sauces for the served course
have been brought to the table. Repeat for each course. And
don't forget to mark your table in between each course.

The Two-Minute Rule applies here; you must circle back
to your table approximately two minutes after the food has
been served to make sure the customers received the food
they ordered, the food meets their expectations, and that
they are enjoying themselves. Of course, make sure they
have had a chance to taste their food. Again, reading the
table is very important.

Clearing the Table

When everybody at your table is done eating, you can begin clearing from the right of your guest (when possible). Remove all dirty plates and silverware. Take the opportunity to remove empty glasses, empty bottles of wine, unused utensils, sugar wrappers, and any other unnecessary objects. Crumb your table. During your final clear, salt and pepper shakers should also be removed from the table before dessert. The table should be bare and neat except for the water glasses and any other glasses that still have a beverage in it.

Dessert Time

Bring the dessert menus and distribute them as described in the section "Approach the Table" (page 40) Make recommendations, talk about a special dessert, if any, or the ice cream and sorbet flavors, if they are not listed. This is also the time to ask if the customer would like some tea, coffee, espresso, cappuccino, latte, macchiato or mocha, or an after-meal drink. It never hurts to keep offering and selling. They may well say "no," but they could also say "yes." Don't miss an opportunity to make a sale.

Last Act, Check Time

When you observe that your customers are done eating, approach the table and ask if they are finished enjoying their meal. (Never use verbiage like, "Are you done working on your meal?" They are not working but enjoying.) Ask if they would like anything else. If they say no, then you can bring the check. You can drop the check with the table's host (the person who booked the reservation), or a guest who requests it, or simply place it in the middle of the table.

At this point, observe your table. They will either place a credit card or cash in the check presenter, on a tray, in a glass, or whatever your restaurant uses. Return to the table, pick up the check presenter and say "Thank you." {TIP} *If they pay with cash, count the money immediately in front of the customer, so there is no confusion.* Bring back the exact change and thank them again. If they pay with a credit card, run the card through the POS and bring the check with the credit card voucher back, along with a working pen. Keep in mind that there is nothing more frustrating than a server who gives you a pen which is dry to sign your credit card voucher at the end of a wonderful meal. You could go from a 20% tip to 15% or less in a split second, just by making this common mistake. That would be a shame after all this hard work, wouldn't it? {TIP} *On the other hand, writing "Thank you!" on top of the credit card voucher has a great chance to increase your tip.*

Even though you are busy, try to pick up the paid check before the guest leaves your table. There are a couple of reasons for this: you want to make sure they left the right credit card voucher (the one with the tip and the signature) in the check presenter, and you do not want to miss a last occasion to bid your guests farewell and to let them know that you are looking forward to them coming back. Remember that you worked hard on this table, so check time is very important—no room for mistakes here. You want to reap the benefits of your hard work.

Lastly, if you have time, help your busser clear and reset your table, picking up something besides your tip!

Tip Time

The first thing to say about Tip Time is that it is done differently in all restaurants. In the U.S., your tip is most often the main source of your earnings. The average tip amount is 15% of the bill (before tax), though many satisfied guests will tip more, while others may tip less.

There are two types of tipped employees: the primary tip employees who are the waiters and bartenders, and then the secondary tip employees, also referred to as "support staff" who are the bussers, buffers, baristas, food runners and hosts. The manager, or the bartender, pays out the primary tip employees first, who then give a percentage of their tips to the secondary tip employees.

There are different methods for tipping out. Some establishments include tips in their employees' paychecks, others will tip out after each shift, while others may tip out but once a week. Check with your manager to see how this is done in your restaurant.

2.5

SEQUENCE OF SERVICE SUMMARY

1. Approach and then greet the table.
2. Give menus (if not done by host).
3. Serve water.
4. Take beverage order, ring up, pick up at bar and serve.
5. Take food order.
6. Input into POS for the kitchen.
7. Serve the bread.
8. Mark the table.
9. Run the appetizer.
10. Make sure all is okay with your customers. (Two-Minute Rule)
11. Clear the table.
12. Re-mark.
13. Run the main course.
14. Make sure all is okay with your customers. (Two-Minute Rule)
15. Clear the table.
16. Re-mark.
17. Bring the dessert menu.
18. Take the dessert, coffee, and after-meal drink orders.
19. Serve the dessert, coffee, and after-meal drinks.
20. Final clear. Remove all unnecessary pieces of flatware, glassware, etc.
21. Ask the customer if they would like anything else.
22. Present the check.
23. Thank the guest.
24. Pick up payment and process.
25. Bring change back if cash, or credit card vouchers.
26. Have customer sign and leave correct voucher.
27. Bid farewell and thank your customer again.
28. Reset your table.

NOTES

SECTION 3
TOOLS OF THE TRADE

3.1 GLASSWARE

Water Glass

All Purpose Wine Glass

Bordeaux Glass

Burgundy Glass

Champagne Coupe

Champagne Flute

3.1 GLASSWARE

High Ball Glass

Low Ball Glass

Snifter

Martini Glass

Beer Glass

Beer Mug

3.2 KNIFEWARE

Steak Knife   Fish Knife   Butter Knife   Cheese Knife

3.3 SILVERWARE

Salad   Main Course   Main Course   Soup   Dessert
Fork   Fork   Knife   Spoon   Spoon

3.4 SEAFOODWARE

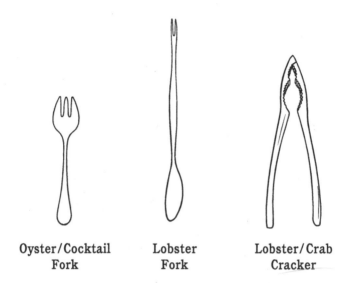

Oyster/Cocktail
Fork

Lobster
Fork

Lobster/Crab
Cracker

3.5 OTHER ESSENTIAL TOOLS

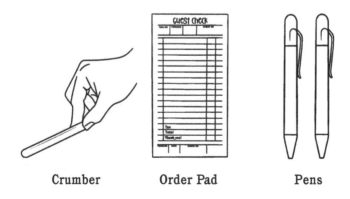

Crumber

Order Pad

Pens

3.6 COFFEE & TEA SERVICE

Coffee Pot

Tea Pot

Coffee / Tea Mug

Coffee / Tea Cup & Saucer

Espresso Cup

Creamer

3.7 WINE TOOLS

Wine Trivet

Wine Opener

Wine Key

Wine Bucket

Decanter / Carafe

SECTION 4

ON WINE

Wine, Wine, Wine!!!

A lot of things have been said about it, a lot of things have been written about it. So much information has been offered up to the general public about wine that it's no wonder that a lot of people are confused and don't really know what to do. My goal is not to make a "Wine Snob" out of you, but to give you the minimum amount of information that will allow you to navigate the subject with confidence.

First, How is Wine Made?

Wine is the fermented juice of pressed grapes. This juice contains sugar. When you add yeast (chemical or natural) to it, fermentation occurs, and the combination of yeast and sugar produces alcohol. And *voilá*, here we go—let's have a toast! Wine can be fermented in barrels, often made of oak. French or American oak are the usual preference. Wine can also be fermented in large stainless steel containers.

After fermentation, wines are filtered to remove yeasts that may cause sediment. It is then bottled, corked, and a capsule or a wax seal is put over the cork. These days, screw caps are becoming more common, officially known as a "Stelvin cap." A label, which is the wine's ID, tells you where the wine comes from (appellation), its alcohol content (as a percentage), its vintage (the year the wine was made), the country of origin, the name of the producer, and the varietal (the type of wine it is). (See illustration on page 75.) The bottle might have all this information on one front label or divided between a front and back label.

Of course, these are just the basics, as it takes much more to make wine. If you aspire to become a winemaker, I would recommend checking out the University of California Davis' Department of Viticulture & Enology.

4.1 WHAT KIND OF WINES ARE OUT THERE?

White, rosé and red, are the most common colors. Still and sparkling are the carbonation choices. A wine is "fortified" when brandy is added to it, like port, and a dessert wine when the grape is left to dry on the vine, producing a sweeter wine. Botrytized wines are also sweet, but with the flavor imparted by the presence of the so-called "noble rot."

Wine is produced all over the world, and thousands of different grapes (varietals) exist. But you'll only see a few on most restaurants' wine lists.

For the whites, some of the most common varietals are chardonnay, sauvignon blanc, chenin blanc, or albariño.

For the reds, varietals such as cabernet sauvignon, merlot, cabernet franc, syrah, grenache, tempranillo, zinfandel, pinot noir, sangiovese, and nebbiolo would be the most common on a wine list.

Most rosés, will typically be made from pinot noir, grenache or blends.

You will discover the world of sparkling wines like the famous Champagne from the namesake region of France, usually made with chardonnay, pinot noir or pinot meunier in white or rosé (seldom red, except sparkling wines like Lambrusco from Italy).

You will become familiar with words like "Old World" wines, which are basically wines that come from old Europe. All other wines, coming from anywhere else, are called "New World" wines.

Wines have different styles due to the climate, different soil types the grapes are grown in and different farming and winemaking practices. Words commonly associated with wine are *dry, big, oaky, buttery, light, medium, and full bodied.* The best way to learn about wine is to taste, taste, taste (but don't forget to spit it out). In between tasting, you must read, read, read. An excellent book I would, once again, recommend is: *Great Wines Made Simple*, by Master Sommelier Andrea Immer Robinson.

4.2 WHEN FOOD MEETS WINE, AND VICE VERSA

Food and wine pairing is a big challenge for a lot of people! Very scary, kinda like walking through a cemetery on Halloween night. Come on, get a hold of yourself! This is not rocket science, nothing to get hung up on, just read carefully.

Once upon a time, in the Old World, people had food. Food was, and still is, regional. Those same people made wine, and guess what, they all had the brilliant idea to make wine that suited the food they ate. In some instances they went as far as using the wine of their region to cook their food. Do you know why a Beef Bourguignon tastes so good when paired with a bold pinot noir, such as Nuit-St Georges from Burgundy? Because Bourguignon means "The Burgundian Way"—a beef cooked with a pinot noir that is mainly grown in Burgundy ... what a novel idea! That is not to say that other red wines would not pair well with this Beef Bourguignon, such as a nice Côtes-du-Rhone or Bordeaux, but let's keep it simple. Regional food paired with regional wine is a good start.

Another way for a restaurant to pair food and wine well is for the person in charge of the wine list to note wine selections which complement food items right on the menu—very easy.

Here are some wine and food pairing basics that can be used as a general rule of thumb:

- Champagne goes well with everything, this is the wine of the gods, period.
- White wines — fish or seafood.
- Red wines — meat.
- Sweeter wines — spicy food.
- Sweet wines — dessert and cheese.
- High acidity wines — richer food, especially dishes with a lot of butter or fat content. Raw oysters, a salty food, and sauvignon blanc are also very good friends.
  {TIP} *You know when a wine has a high acidity level because it makes you salivate, like when you put lemon on your tongue.*
- Low acidity wines — high acidity foods.

Of course, you will encounter some exceptions, but these are good, basic guidelines that will make you informed and well-appreciated. A good food and wine pairing is like a marriage made in heaven; they complement each other, they make each other better, they enlighten your palate and help you reach "Culinary Nirvana!"

4.3 WINE SERVICE

Taking the Wine Order

Different situations can occur: It can be as simple as the customer already knowing which wine they plan to drink with their meal to the customer who does not know and needs some recommendations and advice. In any case, do not be a "Wine Snob"—make your recommendations and explanations as simple as possible. Avoid using terms they will not understand. If you do say something your customer does not understand, kindly explain what it means.

The rule of thumb here is: Do not intimidate the guests—be humble! Your wine knowledge is very valuable to them; it is inappropriate to make them feel ignorant.

Some questions to ask your customers:
- What do they usually like to drink?
- Price Range: how much do they want to spend on wine?
- Preferences: Likes and dislikes: white or red? Sweet or dry? Light, medium or full-bodied? Young or old? Most important of all: Ask them (if you don't already know) what they plan to eat.

Once all the pertinent questions have been answered, proceed in recommending a few wines in their price range which, to the best of your knowledge, will complement their food.

When to Take a Wine Order?

When first approaching the table, after greeting the guests, ask the customer if they would like a cocktail or if they'd like to start with some wine. Keep in mind that wine should always be served before the food hits the table.

Different scenarios:
- Customers want to start with wine. Place the order, pick up and come back to serve the wine.
- Customers want to start with cocktails. Take the wine order when they place their food order.
- Each time they finish their wine, ask them if they would like to have more.
- Some customers prefer a different wine for each course. Make sure to get their orders in early enough to serve each particular wine before the course they want to drink it with arrives.

How to Take a Wine Order

Approach the person holding the wine list or the table's host and ask if they would like to have wine with their meal. If they have already decided on a particular wine, make sure to repeat the order back to them. If there is any uncertainty at all, have the person who is ordering point to the selected wine on the wine list.

Decanting or Carafing

Some of the wines on your list may be offered both by the glass and by the bottle. Always confirm with the guest which they prefer. When the guest has made their selection, it is time to pop the big "D" question: Does the customer want the wine decanted? If the customer has ordered a red wine of an older vintage and would like to separate the sediment, decanting helps. If the wine is young and assertive and needs some breathing, then we "carafe" it. It is important to ask this question when taking the order so that you can gather the tools necessary to decant or carafe the wine.

How to Serve Wine

Once the wine is ordered, set the table with the appropriate glasses and wine trivet or ice bucket for the wine bottle. Stand on the right side of the person who ordered it, and proceed with opening it (see pages 71-74). Wine, as with all beverages, must be poured from the right.

When done pouring, place the bottle in front of the person who ordered it, on the wine trivet with the label facing the guest. If wine has been decanted or carafed, place the decanter on the right side of the bottle. White wine can be placed in a wine bucket, if the guest wishes to keep it cold.

4.4 HOW TO OPEN A BOTTLE OF WINE

Equipment: napkin, wine opener, wine coaster, trivet

1. Present the bottle to the guest, standing to his or her right. Clearly state the brand name, the vintage, the varietal, the appellation, and the designated vineyard (if available). A clean napkin should be over your forearm, making sure the backside is slightly damp.

2. Switch the bottle to your left hand. Practice being able to operate the wine opener with one hand. Flip open the knife on the opener. Running the knife along the bottom of the lip of the bottle, cut one half of the foil from the front, flip knife and cut the foil on the opposite side.

3. Continue to hold the bottle by the neck, with the label still facing the customer. With the knife and your thumb pressing on the top, using an upward motion, peel off the cut foil, peeling towards yourself. Close the knife and put the closed knife and the cut foil in your pocket.

4.4 HOW TO OPEN A BOTTLE OF WINE

4. Use the damp side of the napkin to clean the mouth of the bottle. Wipe clean any debris showing inside the mouth.

5. Open the corkscrew: After inspecting the cork, pierce the center of the cork with the screw.

6. With label still facing the guest, screw into the cork.

4.4 HOW TO OPEN A BOTTLE OF WINE

7. Placing the lever against the lip of the bottle, push up on the handle to remove the cork.

8. Hold the cork next to the neck of the bottle with your left hand. Unscrew the corkscrew from the cork.

9. Flip the corkscrew closed. Ask the guest if they would like to inspect the cork. If so, place the cork in front of them on a wine trivet. If not, place the cork in your pocket.

4.4 HOW TO OPEN A BOTTLE OF WINE

10. Switch the bottle to your right hand, with the label still facing the guest. Wipe the lip of the bottle with the damp napkin.

11. Pour 2 oz. of wine into the host's glass to taste. After pouring, twist the bottle slightly to avoid drips.

12. Wipe the mouth of the bottle after each pour.

1. Product Name: Winery or individual brand

2. Vintage: Year the grapes were harvested

3. Varietal: Type of grape predominantly used; must have 75% of the varietal to carry the name

4. Appellation: Where the grapes were grown

5. Chemical preservative

6. Alcohol Content: Percentage of alcohol

SECTION 5
CONCLUSION

Knowledge is power. When correctly equipped with the tools and the knowledge to create an exceptional dining experience, you will feel a new sense of comfort on the stage that is the dining room floor. Becoming fluid in the art of service is attainable through authenticity, kindness, a desire to serve, and a continuous thirst for knowledge. The culinary world is an exciting one, full of color, flavors, chatter and guests who have come to share their experience with you.

* A note on post-COVID serving. The restaurant world has been hit hard by the pandemic. Some restaurants have been able to survive, but many small, mom-and-pop establishments have been forced to close.

As we start to re-open, having the know-how to serve guests with finesse and confidence will help our industry get up and running more quickly.

I'm hoping that this handbook will assist in this endeavor, making life easier for restaurant owners, managers and waiters and enhancing the experience of our guests, the diners.

SECTION 6

GLOSSARY

86

This number means that you are out of an item from the menu or wine list.

86 Board

The board on which all items that are 86 (unavailable) are reported. Usually this board is in the kitchen or in the wait station (especially for wine or bar items).

A La Carte

When each item on the menu is sold and priced individually.

A La Mode

When a dish, usually a dessert, is served with ice cream.

Back of the House

The ensemble of people who work in the kitchen (executive chef, chef, sous-chef, line cook, dishwasher).

Back Waiter

The position that assists the front waiter in all their needs, transmits the order to the kitchen, marks the table, serves the cocktails, opens the wine, runs the food, etc. Restaurants using this front/back waiter system seldom use bussers. The back waiter puts the bread on the tables, takes care of refills (water, coffee, etc.), clears and resets the tables.

B&B Plate

Bread and butter plate. A small plate, usually placed on the left side of the fork.

Bespoke

Custom-made, personalized. Often used to designate a VIP. Some restaurant or hotels have two levels, Bespoke 1 and Bespoke 2, meaning that they require different levels of attention.

Buff

The action of polishing glassware, silverware or china after it has been washed.

Buffer

Person who buffs/polishes silverware and glassware.

Busser

Person who helps the waiter with their section, sets up tables, serves water, iced tea, soda or coffee, puts bread on the table, refills drinks when necessary, helps clear and re-mark tables. Does not take orders.

Cakeage Fee

The amount of money charged when someone brings their own cake to a restaurant and requests the restaurant cut and serve it.

Call Drink or Call

When someone orders a drink by name. Three categories exist for drinks: "Well" the most affordable, "Call" will cost you a little more and "Premium" may cost you a lot more, depending on the selection.

Camper

Refers to guests who overstay their time in your section, even after the check has been settled.

Carafing Wine

The action of quickly pouring a young and assertive wine into a carafe in order to aerate and help it develop its aroma, or "open up."

Centerpiece

Decoration (flowers, candelabra, ornaments), placed in the center of the table.

Charcuterie

Selection of cold cuts: sausage, salami, ham, paté, etc. served as an appetizer.

Charger

Large plate (usually 12–inch) placed in table set-up, between the silverware, under the napkin.

Check

Bill that is brought to the customer at the end of the meal.

Check Average

The average amount of money spent per person. Let's say that a table of four spent $100. Your check average (per person) would be $25.

Clear a Table

The action to remove glassware, silverware, and plates from a table.

Clip

Serving utensils for a shared plate.

Comp or On-the-House

Short for complimentary. When you take care of a guest's drink, food or corkage fee without charge. If you make an ordering mistake and the item is made, you will need to take it off the check by comping it.

Corkage Fee

The amount of money charged per bottle of wine that the customer brings into the restaurant and the waiter opens (also called service charge).

Corked Wine

Slang term to describe a wine that has gone bad. Technically, this means that the cork, and therefore the wine, has been contaminated with Trichloranisole or TCA. A corked wine has a damp aroma or flavor, like a wet dog or wet cardboard.

Coursing

To course a meal is to send the food items separately to a table. Example: if a table orders five appetizer courses to share at once, it is proper service to ask them if they want those items to be sent to the table together or separately, meaning one by one.

Cover

Refers to a guest or customer. A reservation for eight people translates to eight covers.

Crumb a Table

The action to remove all the debris, bread crumbs, etc. from a table, usually using a tool called a crumber.

Decanting Wine

The action to slowly pour a wine into a carafe or decanter in order to separate the juice from the sediment.

Detail a Table

The action of keeping a table current by removing any unnecessary pieces of glassware, china, flatware or silverware during the guest's meal.

Deuce

Party or table of two people.

Dine-and-Dash

When a guest sneaks out without paying the bill for their meal.

Door or Front Door

Refers to the host.

Drop the Food

To place the food you picked up in the kitchen in front of your guest.

English Service

Also called Silver Service. Food service at the table. Waiter transfers food from a serving dish to each individual guest's plate. It is performed by a waiter using a service fork and spoon from the diner's left side.

Expeditor

Person who expedites the food. The expeditor usually stands in front of the kitchen line and directs the food runners to the appropriate table with the appropriate food. The expeditor also facilitates communication between the kitchen and the wait staff.

Family Meal

Meal served to staff, often served family style, in the kitchen before service begins.

Family Style

A way to serve the food on large platters that is set in the middle of the table for the customers or employees to share.

Fire an Order

Action to ask the kitchen to cook the food you ordered for your guests, usually using a POS; can also be a "verbal fire."

Flatware

Refers to eating ustensils such as forks, spoons and serving tools.

Floor

Short for dining room area.

Floor Map

Before each shift, the MOD prepares a floor map that shows the waiters' serving sections. This floor map is usually posted at the host's podium.

Fly or Fly an Order

Term used when you need an order to be fired immediately because you forgot to order the food, or you made a mistake and you need the food as soon as possible, or the customers are in a hurry.

Food Runner

Person who delivers the food from the kitchen to the table. This person does not take any orders, they just run food, communicating with the kitchen, the waiters, and the bar about any food-related changes or any problems that may occur regarding the delivery of the food.

Front of the House

Ensemble of people who work on the floor (managers, hosts, bartenders, waiters, wine waiters or sommeliers, bussers).

Front Waiter

Some places work with a front and back waiter system. Each team is in charge of a section. The front waiter doesn't usually leave the section. He explains the menu, takes the orders and then communicates all the information to the back waiter.

Glassware

Ensemble of all glasses used in a restaurant or bar: martini glasses, champagne flutes, coupes, snifters, wine glasses, water glasses, etc.

Hands In, Hands Out

In restaurant lingo, it means to never go empty-handed. Always carry dirty items when going to the dish pit in the kitchen and always bring back clean items when returning to the floor.

Hand Sell

Items that are not on the menu, wine list, or specials, but are available at the restaurant to be sold.

Hollowware

Tea pots, coffee pots, water pitcher, etc.

Host or Hostess

Person who answers the phone, greets the people at the door, takes and checks reservations, brings guests to their table, and gives them the menu and wine list. They will let the waiter in charge know about any special requests from, or information about, the guests (such as birthdays, anniversaries, VIP parties, etc.). Today this position is referred to as the gender neutral host.

House Account

Some restaurants allow their regular customers to have a house account; which allows them to "sign" for meals and receive a bill once a month.

Liner

Plate that you put under another dish (like when serving a bowl of soup or pasta), usually covered with a paper napkin to avoid slippage.

Mark or Re-mark a Table

Action to bring to the table all silverware or glassware necessary for the next course after the used ones have been cleared and the table crumbed.

Marking Tray

Tray, usually rectangular in shape and lined with a napkin, used to help carry silverware and B&B plate to mark a table.

Michelin Star

Michelin Stars are a highly regarded rating system used by the Michelin Guide to grade restaurants on their quality. According to the guide, one star signifies "a very good restaurant," two stars are "excellent cooking that is worth a detour," and three stars mean "exceptional cuisine that is worth a special journey." Only the world's greatest dining establishments attain that coveted third star. Thomas Keller's French Laundry in Yountville and Per Se in NYC are two of them.

Mise en Place

Refers to front of the house set up to be ready for service.

MOD

Manager on duty.

Modifier

Additional options available in your POS system to modify an order. Usually your computer is loaded with modifiers, such as rare, no salt, sauce on the side, etc. They allow more detailed communication with the kitchen and bar and save a lot of time.

Neat

When a drink is served neat, it is served right out of the bottle, without any ice, garnish or being blended with anything.

No show

When a party has a reservation but does not show up. Some restaurants charge a per person fee to make up for the loss of business.

Noble Rot

Grey fungus affecting overripe wine grapes resulting in increased sugar and flavor content.

Order Pad

Small pad where you write your order.

Party

Group of people coming to eat at the restaurant.

Patron

A person who gives support (patronizes) to a business such as a restaurant. Another word for guest.

Plated

Food individually put on plates in the kitchen.

POS

Point of Sale. This is a computer system designed specifically for restaurants. Popular systems are: Aloha, Micros, Positouch, Square, Squirrel, and Toast.

Position Numbers

Numbers assigned to guests at the same table. For example, some restaurants decide that for each table, the guest turning their back to the entrance door will be in position one. From there, we move clockwise with the person to their left in position two and so on.

Premium

The highest and often most expensive liquor selection available.

PX or PPX

Restaurant industry code for Very Important Person or V.I.P. Due to the need to communicate on the floor within earshot of customers, some restaurants took the habit of referring to their VIP as PX. Everyone knows what VIP means but customers do not know or understand what PX means. PX stands for *Personne Extraordinaire* (extraordinary person) and PPX for *Personne Particulierement Extraordinaire* (particulary extraordinary person).

Read a Table

The action of observing your guests to determine their needs: how fast they eat, when to place their order, if they need attention, etc.

Refill

The action of refilling a water glass, iced tea, coffee cup or other beverage. Refills are usually free.

Rocks or On the Rocks

A drink that is served with ice. Rocks refers to ice.

Rollup

Eating utensils that are rolled up in napkins.

Rover

Person used sometimes in busy restaurants to clear and reset tables.

Run the Food

The action to pick up the food in the kitchen and bring it to your guest. No need to run, just walk to your table at a good pace, with your head up and a sense of purpose.

Section

The number of tables given to a waiter represent a section. Each waiter has a section, which can be of two, three, four, five or more tables, all depending on your restaurant.

Server Assistant

Another word often used in high-end restaurants for a busser.

Service Plate

A plate (12" or larger) that is used as a base plate for soup bowls and salad plates and removed before the main course. Also called a charger or liner.

Set a Table

Action to place all the items (plates, glassware, silverware) on a table in order to be ready for a meal.

Share Plates

Plates that you put in front of the patrons to allow them to share their food.

Shift

Waiter's workday, can be lunch shift or evening shift, and in some restaurants, it can be split shift, which means you work lunch and then come back for dinner (also referred to as a "double".)

Side Jobs

Tasks required before, during and after service to help the team perform—for example but not limited to, brewing coffee, making iced tea, folding napkins, setting up the bread station, filling salt and pepper shakers, filling water pitchers, etc.

Silverware

Cutlery made or coated with silver. In restaurants, all knives, spoons, forks, teaspoons, etc. are called silverware even if they are not coated with silver.

Slammed, To Be Slammed

When the door seats two, three or more tables at the same time in your section and you are overwhelmed.

Sommelier

Also called Wine Waiter, a Sommelier is a person who specializes in wine, and makes wine and food pairing recommendations.

SOS

"Sauce on the Side"

Specials

Daily menu additions, sometimes printed on the menu, sometimes verbal (in which case, you have to tell the customer what they are).

Split

When your guest wants their shared dish split for them in the kitchen.

Star or VIP Party

Party that your restaurant wants to treat with special attention for whatever reason (famous people, partner or investors in the business, regulars, etc.).

Tab

Another word for the check or bill.

Table Number

In most restaurants each table has a number you must learn before starting to work. This is used as a reference number when ordering.

The Line

This is the kitchen line (also called the pass) where you pick up the food for your guest.

Tender Care

In restaurant lingo, this is a code word for a difficult customer.

Temp or Temperature

It is very Important to ask your guests how they want their meat cooked. Usually temperature is taken for red meat, and sometimes for certain cuts of pork and veal, as well as fish. Here are the temperatures from lowest to highest: black & blue (barely cooked, just turned and returned), blue, rare, medium rare, medium, medium well and well done.

Tip

Amount of money given to the waiter by the customer. Usually 15 percent of the total bill. It can be 20 percent or more. There is no limit, it all depends on how much the customer appreciates your service. Another good reason to be good—the more you give it your best, the more money you make.

Top

Usually preceded by a number (4 top, 6 top, etc.) This is the number of set-ups you need to have on a table, corresponding to the number of guests. For example, the door will tell you, "I need a 4 top on this table."

Tray

Usually round in shape; trays in restaurants are useful to carry glasses, silverwares, drinks and a lot of other things from point A to point B. It is important to carry items in a clean and professional manner.

Turn a Table

Amount of times a table is used for different customers during a set time, such as dinner.

Two-Minute Rule

Rule stating that you should greet your guests within two minutes of them being seated in your section and return to check on them two minutes after the food has been dropped.

Umami

Used to describe that "perfect" taste!

Up

Drinks shaken or stirred and served without ice.

Void

When an Item Is deleted from a guest check. The item (food or drink) has not been made and therefore does not need to be comped but instead, voided, as there is no product lost.

Wait Station

This is the hub of Waiters' World, the place in the restaurant where the waiters and bussers find whatever they need in order to do their job: coffee, tea, butter, bread, silverware, glassware, plates, computers, etc. This place is usually concealed from the guests' eyes.

Walk-In

A guest who comes to the restaurant without a reservation.

Walk-In refrigerator

Large refrigerator, usually located outside or in the kitchen, used to store the food. Favorite place for waiters or line cooks to go scream or cry when they are stressed.

Water Chart

Some high-end and Michelin Star restaurants use a water chart to track the type of water that each guest consumes to avoid the staff having to ask every time they want to serve and refill their glass.

Waive

Action to waive a fee, such a corkage, cakeage or a room fee.

Weeded—To Be Weeded or In the Weeds

When you are so busy or slammed, that you cannot handle the situation.

Well Drink

The most affordable liquor selection. When a guest orders a cocktail without specifying which base liquor he wants, the bartender will use the "well liquor," which is the most affordable.

Wine Snob

Expression used to describe a pretentious wine enthusiast who is self-important due to their "immense wine knowledge" causing others to feel inferior or irritated.

Wine Trivet

Also known as a coaster. Saucer that you place under a bottle of wine.

NOTES

QUIZ

1. What does "Hands In, Hands Out" mean?

☐ a. To always have your hands busy carrying things to and from the kitchen.

☐ b. To keep your hands in your pockets until the customer initiates a handshake.

☐ c. To move your hands on and off the table in a rhythmical way.

2. What is the meaning of MOD?

☐ a. Master of Dining

☐ b. Manager on Duty

☐ c. Manager Off Duty

3. Which varietal is used in white wine?

☐ a. Cabernet Sauvignon

☐ b. Chardonnay

☐ c. Pinot Noir

4. We do our Side Jobs:

☐ a. To get ready to open for the next shift.

☐ b. Throughout our shift.

☐ c. Both of the above.

QUIZ

5. What is the Charger?

☐ a. A device placed on the table to charge phones.

☐ b. A large plate placed between the silverware, under the napkin.

☐ c. A device used for processing credit cards.

6. To Course a Meal means:

☐ a. To run with a meal.

☐ b. To bring each dish, one at a time.

☐ c. To rush guests through their meal.

7. What does POS stand for?

☐ a. Pre-Order Service

☐ b. Pour Over Sauce

☐ c. Point of Sale

8. Serving Open means:

☐ a. Serving from the right with your right hand and from the left with your left hand.

☐ b. Allowing space between you and the guest.

☐ c. Both of the above.

QUIZ

9. When a guest pays the check with cash:

☐ a. You count the cash immediately, in front of the guest.

☐ b. You take it and return with change immediately.

☐ c. You wait until the guest leaves to count the cash.

10. What does Marking a Table mean?

☐ a. Writing the table number on the table with a pen.

☐ b. Bringing to the table all silverware or glassware necessary for the next course after the used ones have been cleared and the table crumbed.

☐ c. Letting the kitchen know that someone at a table has food allergies.

SCORE: _____

Answers: 1a, 2b, 3b, 4c, 5b, 6b, 7c, 8c, 9a, 10b

NOTES

NOTES

A FINAL THOUGHT

Thank you for taking the time to
study this guide to
the art of waiting tables.
I hope you have learned something new
that will make your work more
enjoyable and fulfilling.

If you are so inclined, please consider
revisiting the website where you purchased
this book and leave a review.

Your suggestions and comments are most welcome.
Please send them to:
info@welcometowaitersworld.com

ACKNOWLEDGEMENTS

Book Design & Editing:
Barbara Schwartz / Arielle Hoachuck
zoomonby.com

Book Drawings: Julian Thomas
fiverr.com/weedstation

Wine Opening Drawings: Cort Sinnes
artworkarchive.com/profile/a-cort-sinnes